JAPAN

EXPLORING THE LAND OF THE RISING SUN

The Ultimate Guide to Visiting Japan

Ambreen Hameed

Table of Contents

INTRODUCTION

Let's face it. We are all fascinated with Japan. A country which is so technologically advanced isn't something that you can just ignore! But, when you read more about Japan and its culture, you'll find that there are many other interesting and equally as fascinating facts about this country.

Visiting Japan would probably make you feel that you are living in the future, especially when you are in the busy streets of Tokyo. But, if you visit an old traditional town or village away from the capital, you will experience an entirely different way of life.

Of course, Tokyo is one of the most famous cities in the world, with neon-lights and sushi bars aplenty! Most people who come and visit the capital are usually overwhelmed by the experience they've just had. Head away from there, and you'll see rice paddies, snowy mountains, locals who will do all they can to help, and the most idyllic scene you'll set your eyes on. Put simply, Japan is a once in a lifetime destination, and the fact you're reading this book tells us that you're thinking of heading there yourself.

Great choice!

This book is going to tell you all you need to know about your upcoming adventure and provide you all the important information to help you plan your time as well as your finances. Japan is a country like no other, even from its neighboring countries. They have their own unique in language, currency, history, and culture. Traveling to Japan could be one of the best travel experiences for you.

Why is Japan called 'The Land of the Rising Sun'?

Before we get into the good stuff, we need to address a burning question. Why Japan is called 'The Land of the Rising Sun'?

This is where it gets complicated. There are many different theories as to why, and nobody is 100% set on the right one. Despite that, most people agree that it is because the geographical location of Japan is close to where the sun rises across the whole of Asia. Within the region, the ancient Chinese civilizations basically created everything, from culture to language, and everything else derived from there over the centuries. When the Chinese looked towards Japan, they needed to look east, and that in itself is closer to where the sun rises, hence the name.

Regardless of arguments over Japan's nickname, there is a lot to explore in this extremely beautiful country. So, enough chatter, let's dive in to the good stuff!

Chapter 1:
WELCOME TO JAPAN

The fact you're thinking about visiting Japan means that you are looking for an adventure, and it will certainly be an experience that you will always remember. There are so many things to see and do in Japan, and you will need to make a lot of room in your phone memory for all the amazing photos that you'd want to take when you get there. Japan is one of the countries that has many Instagrammable spots, so better come prepared with your OOTD!

Before you start planning your trip, there are a few basic information that you need to know. This chapter is going to give you some interesting facts about Japan.

What you should realize is that Japan is not like any other country. If you're simply visiting Tokyo, you're going to need a vacation afterward to get over it! For that reason, traveling to other places while in Japan is definitely a must-do; explore so you will see and experience more things about the Japanese culture. Don't forget to visit the small towns or the more serene part of this beautiful country.

Just to give you an idea of how popular Japan is these days, a huge 19.7 million people visited Japan in 2018, and the world's fascination to this remarkable country shows no sign of slowing down! So, if you are already excited to visit Japan, then you'd better have an idea of the important things about the place.

Quick and Interesting Facts You Need to Know

Before visiting Japan, there are a few basic things you need to know, like the following:

- Capital: Tokyo
- Population: 126.8 million
- Size: 377,972 square kilometers
- Currency: Japanese Yen
- Religion: Shinto and Buddhism
- Language: Japanese, although in large towns and cities you will find locals who can speak English

Japan is an island prefecture, and it is made up of four main island masses, including Kyushu, Hokkaido, Honshu (where you'll find Tokyo), and Shikoku. Overall, Japan is located in the Far East of Asia, and it is surrounded by the Pacific Ocean on the eastern side and the Sea of Okhotsk, the East China Sea, the Sea of Japan, and the Philippine Sea on its other sides.

When you first start to read about Japan you'll see that it has many quirks, and probably many things will make you shake your head in bemusement; that's one of the wonderful things about this country!

Here are some interesting and fun facts about Japan:

- In total, Japan has more than 6800 islands, most of which are totally uninhabited
- Anime – is a form of animated film and TV show which is popular in Japan
- You will find square watermelons in Japan! These are considered easier to pack and store
- Japan is home to 5.52 million vending machines, and they don't only sell foods ....
- The McDonalds icon Ronald McDonald is called Donald McDonald in Japan because of the lack of an 'R' sound in the language
- You cannot use a public bathing house or even a hot spring if you have tattoos; because these are associated with gangs!
- Sumo wrestling is big business here, and you have to go and experience the show!
- It's not rude if you hear someone slurping very loudly when eating noodles, it is their way of appreciating the food
- The entire Greater Tokyo area is considered the largest metropolitan area in the world
- Despite that, Tokyo is actually very expensive and is the second most expensive city on Earth
- You will see more elderly people than children, due to fewer couples having kids
- You'll find the oldest people in the world in Okinawa; aged 116 and 117 years old!
- Japan is known to be the most earthquake-prone countries in the world, with around 1500 a year; don't panic, however, many of these are tiny
- If you're traveling by train and a member of staff literally pushes you inside, don't worry, they're paid to do that. Trains in Japan are so busy, especially in Tokyo that space is at a premium!
- You're unlikely to be allowed into a public bath or a hot spring if you have tattoos; these are sometimes considered to be associated with gangs

- Mount Fuji is the highest point of Japan, at 3776 meters high

The Dos and Don'ts of Visiting Japan

Japanese culture is so vibrant and unique that at first, it can be difficult to figure out what you should and shouldn't do. You are likely to make a mistake, especially if you have not read up about their culture and etiquette. Thankfully, Japanese people are very understanding, and know that you are not being rude, you are just not aware of them! To help you avoid making mistakes that may inadvertently insult someone, let's check out the dos and don'ts when visiting Japan. These can help you learn more about their unique culture.

The Dos

- You should always take off your shoes if you're visiting someone's home, but there are a few other places where this rule applies. Japanese have simplified manners, and whenever you see a raised entrance to a building, that is a sign that you need to take off your shoes! Another sign is a shoe rack outside
- When you meet someone and say 'hello', bow down, rather than shaking hands. The lower you bow, the most respect you are showing to that person
- Learn a few words of the language, no matter how difficult it might seem! At the end of this chapter, you'll find a few useful words you can learn
- If you are giving a gift, or receiving one, it's important to hold it with both hands
- Always be respectful and dress appropriately when visiting a temple
- Use the water bowl when entering a shrine. You need to wash your hands and rinse your mouth, before spitting it onto the floor

The Don'ts

- Never blow your nose in public or in front of a Japanese person; this is considered super rude!
- Never play around with chopsticks, and only use them when you're eating. Similarly, never leave a pair of chopsticks upright in a rice bowl, and never use your chopsticks to pass food to another person
- Pour your own drink from a shared bottle. For instance, if you are a group and you're sharing a bottle of sake, another person should pour your drink and you should pour theirs
- Never bother with tipping. If you do it, you'll only be given it back
- Never speak on your phone whilst using public transport, and turn it onto silent if you can
- Never bypass the queue. The Japanese are very keen queuers!

Why Should You Visit Japan?

Why? It's because there is no other place on Earth like it! Japan is so different to anywhere else, not only because of their culture and food, but in their language, the beautiful sceneries, and everything about it. Japan never attempts to tone itself down or imitate anyone else. Just by visiting Japan, you are really going on an adventure of a lifetime. And by sampling even a tiny bit of its culture, you will surely learn something new.

Useful Japanese Words to Learn

When you visit Tokyo, you will find some people who can speak English. But, in the small towns and villages, the majority of the people will only be able to speak in Japanese. For that reason, knowing a few words could help you out.

- Hello – Konnichiwa
- Goodbye – Sayonara
- Thank you – Arigatou gozaimasu
- Please – Onegaishimasu

- Excuse me – Sumimasen
- Yes – Hai
- No – Iie (pronounced eee)
- I'm sorry – Gomen nasai
- I don't understand – Wakarimasen
- Can you speak English? – Eigo o hanasemasu ka?

Chapter 2:
JAPAN'S CLIMATE AND WHEN TO VISIT

Surprisingly, Japan's weather has four seasons, which most people don't expect! In many ways that is a great thing, because you can choose the type of weather you want and it's not going to vary too far from averages.

Climate Information You Need to Know

As we've just mentioned, Japan has the four seasons of Spring, Summer, Autumn, and Winter, but because of its close proximity to water (four main islands, remember) and because of the high mountains in certain areas, you're bound to get variations depending upon where you're traveling. The island of Honshu, for example, has what we will call a subtropical climate and that can make it quite humid. This includes Tokyo.

The adverse weather of typhoons tend to hit around August and September if they're going to happen, but May to October is the official span of the rainy season. During this time, you will have prior notice of any adverse weather, and it will normally be strong winds and rain. If typhoons are strong, you will see ferries and planes put on hold until the weather has cleared.

If you're visiting Hokkaido, this is the coldest of all the islands and the one in the furthest north. Here the winters are far longer than the summer and it's not unusual for snow to fall quite heavily at times. With that in mind, if you love skiing, this is the spot for you! Between December and April, you'll find ski resorts packed; yes, Japan has ski resorts!

Okinawa is the hottest of the islands and sits on the furthest south. Summers here are very long and easily average around 32 degrees between May to September.

Let's sum up:

- Spring and autumn are considered the shoulder seasons and are pretty mild regardless of where you go. This is March to May and October to November
- Summer is between June to September and can reach the mid-30s. During this time, make sure you apply your sunscreen and wear a hat
- The summer months are also the rainiest, and it's not impossible to see rain during July and August; make sure you have an umbrella with you
- Typhoon is between May to October, but is likely to happen during August and September

- Winter time is classed as December to the beginning of March and during this time you will see a lot of snow in many areas, especially if you head to Hokkaido

Important Public Holidays and Celebrations

During public holidays and celebrations, you'll find beaches, shopping malls, and other sightseeing spots very, very busy! It is also very likely that public transport is going to be very busy that you need to have someone to push you onto that busy train! In this case, it might be best to avoid some of the more popular spots at this time, but conversely, you'll also get to see a very traditional way of life, where families go out for the day to celebrate.

Here are some notable dates for your reference:

- **1 January – Ganjitsu (New Year's Day).** You'll find that most businesses stay closed until around 3 January, as everyone celebrations the start of a brand new calendar year. New Year is perceived as a fresh start in Japan, and if you have worries on 31 December, the dawn of the new day should wipe them clean.
- **11 February – Kenkoku Kinen No Hi (National Foundation Day).** This is a national day of celebration for the day when Japan was formed. You will see the Japanese flag on view in many places and the Prime Minister will address the nation on TV. This is one day when Japanese people show their pride in their country.
- **3 March – Matsuri (Girl's Festival).** This is the day when parents who are lucky enough to have daughters celebrate their future success and their happiness. You'll find dolls on display in home windows and shops, as well as the peach blossom.
- **20 & 21 March – Shunbun No Hi (Vernal Equinox).** This is the end of winter and the start of spring. You will find many families heading to graveyards to visit their ancestors at this time. This is also a farming celebration, who send their prayers for a successful year's harvest.

- **29 April - Showa No Hi (The Showa Day).** Showa Day is considered a part of the Golden Week, which celebrates a happy and prosperous period in Japanese history. The Showa Era spanned between 1926 and 1989, and you'll find many celebrations going on around the country, especially in the main cities and towns.
- **29 April to 8 May - Golden Week.** From the Showa Day celebrations we enter Golden Week, with various days celebrating periods of Japanese history. This also includes Constitution Day on 3 May, which celebrates the day of the new constitution, back in 1947. In the weeks leading up to Golden Week, children will learn all about Japanese history in far more depth at school, and you'll see the Japanese flag waved in abundance. The last day of Golden Week is also Children's Day, which is dedicated to sons, so they don't miss out after the Girl's Festival!
- **4 May - Midori No Hi (Greenery Day Celebration).** Japan has a day which celebrates the environment and everything that Mother Nature has given us.
- **20 and 21 June - Summer Solstice.** There are no set days off for this celebration, but you will find various events going on during these two days. The summer solstice is considered to be the longest day of the year.
- **Third Monday of July - Umi No Hi (Ocean Day Celebration).** This is a day which celebrates everything the sea gives to Japan, which is vital as it is, an island country! You'll see many celebrations taking place in the coastal regions, as well as even more seafood than usual!
- **11 August - Mountain Day.** This is another celebration of nature, and this time it is dedicated to the mountains. Many people head towards the various peaks on this day to give thanks.
- **Third Monday of September - Keiro No Hi (Respect for the Elderly Day).** Respect is a huge thing in Japanese culture and this particular day is an opportunity to show respect to the elderly members of the family and also within the community. You will

see many young people and children visiting their elderly family members on this day.

- **Second Monday of October - Taiku No Hi (Sports & Health Day).** This is a fairly new celebration which was put in place after the 1964 Olympic Games, which were held in Tokyo. Overall, this is a day to be active and a celebration which places importance on general health and wellbeing. You'll find many people outside playing sports on this day.
- **23 November - Kinro Kansha No Hi (Labor Day Celebration).** During this day, Japan gives thanks to its workers for everything they do for the country's economy, and for keeping everything ticking over nicely.
- **23 December - Tenno Tanjobi (Emperor's Birthday).** The final holiday of the year is the Emperor's Birthday, and again, you'll see lots of flag flying and celebrations across the country.

These are the official holidays, however, there are also some rather obscure celebrations; what else would you expect from Japan? A few of them are listed below.

- **Sapporo Snow Festival.** This is held during the first week of February and as the name suggests, is about everything to do with snow. The event is held in Hokkaido you'll find amazing skiing and snowboarding and some pretty impressive sculptures made of ice too.
- **Okayama Naked Man Festival.** Yes, you did read that right. Held in February, you will find almost 9000 half naked men choosing to fight over sticks, which they deem to be lucky. They are drenched in water, while the sticks were thrown by the crowd. They don't do this for no reason; these sticks are supposed to be extremely lucky for the coming year.
- **Hakata Dontaku Festival.** If you're visiting in May, be sure to head to Fukuoka City, where you'll find parades, flowers, fun, dancing, and all manner of celebrations going on.

- **Yamagata Hanagasa Matsuri.** Head to Yamagata City in August and you'll see dancing in odd straw hats, floats, parades, food, music, and more than 10,000 dancers. It's a wonderful sight to see.
- **Chichibu Yomatsuri.** Head to Chichibu on 3 December for a fantastic evening time festival which is full of wonder. You'll also be privy to one of the best firework displays you'll ever see.

When is the Best Time to Go and Visit Japan?

Most people go to Japan during the spring and autumn season, simply because the weather is good and there is a lesser chance of rain. Tokyo can be extremely hot during the peak summer months, and when you add in possible rain, you get extremely humid conditions. To avoid that, you may want to go there from March to May or October to November as these are considered to be a great time to visit in the big cities. If you want to ski, its winter all the way, late November to February is the best time to visit the island of Hokkaido.

Many people visit Kyoto, Osaka, and even Tokyo during April especially for the beautiful cherry blossoms that bloom every single year. It's a really special sight, and the weather is ideal for checking this out and adding some wonderful photos to your collection! Another fantastic month for photography is October when you will see the unbelievably brightly colored leaves that signal the autumn's arrival.

In terms of when to go to Japan, it's really a personal choice. There isn't a particularly bad time overall, it's more about avoiding rain and humidity, especially in Tokyo, which usually occurs between July and August.

Chapter 3:
TRAVELING TO JAPAN

Japan is very easy to get to these days, and that's great news for anyone who has ever dreamed of heading here. Of course, we're talking about an island nation, you have the option of flying or taking a boat.

Later we will talk about how to get around Japan, as you have several options in that regard. In this chapter, however, we're focusing on how you will travel to get to Japan.

Please take note that all the information contained in this chapter is correct at the time of print, and things do change from time to time especially with regards to visa application, so be sure to check things thoroughly before you buy your ticket, just to be sure!

How to Get to Japan

Well, you have two options, and these are flying or taking a ferry. For now, let's talk about flying.

Traveling to Japan by Air

Japan has several international airports, which are served by major airlines from all over the world. You will find the largest airport in Tokyo. However, Osaka, Nagoya, and Fukuoka also have international airports. Tokyo has two airports, namely Narita Airport and Haneda Airport. Narita is the main airport and is around an hour away from the main city center of Tokyo. You will find the regular train links to the city center, and the airport itself is pretty sleek and modern, with plenty of facilities. You'll also be able to catch domestic flights here, to other parts of Japan. Haneda Airport is around half an hour from the center of Tokyo.

- **Flying from the UK & Ireland** – There are daily direct flights from London to Tokyo which takes about 12 hours. The main airlines are British Airways, Japan Airlines and Virgin.
- **Flying from the USA & Canada** – Again, you can get direct flights from the several USA and Canada cities to Tokyo, Osaka and also Nagoya. The main airlines are Air Canada, ANA, American Airlines, Japan Airlines, United, and Continental. Most USA cities have a direct flight at least once per day. You can expect flying times from anywhere between 15 hours (traveling from New York) to 10 hours (from LA).
- **Flying From Australia & New Zealand** – Again, you will find direct daily flights from these two countries, at between 10 to 12 hours flying time. The main airlines to look out for here are Qantas, Air New Zealand, and Japan Airlines.

Many other European cities have direct daily flights to Tokyo in particular, but you could also think of having indirect flights if you wanted to cut down your travel expense. Please take note that during Golden Week, in particular, ticket rates can be more expensive.

Traveling to Japan by Sea

You can reach Japan from South Korea by boat, with regular ferries every day. These usually leave Busan and Hakaka Ferry Terminal daily, and arrive in Shimonoseki Kokusai Terminal (on the main island) and Osaka Port International Ferry Terminal in the west. You can reach Japan from Busan in around three hours, but if you're heading to Osaka it will take you 12 hours if you use the Kampu Ferry; this is a cheaper option, but obviously slower as a result.

If you're in China, you can also use the ferry going to Japan, but this will take you a good three days. Not the best use of your time! But, if you want to spend some time at sea however, you will find a once-weekly ferry from Shanghai, to Osaka and Kobe, as well as Nagasaki and Fukuoka towards the south.

Visa Information

Because Japan is now a hugely popular country to visit for tourism, most nationalities are able to travel to Japan freely and will receive a visitor visa when they arrive. This lasts for 90 days, which is likely to be enough for most tourists. However, there is also a list of countries which can only stay there for 15 days.

People from these countries are given a 90-day visit when they arrive:

- Australia
- Austria
- Canada
- France
- Germany

- Hong Kong
- Ireland
- Israel
- Italy
- Malaysia
- Mexico
- Most EU countries
- Netherlands
- New Zealand
- Republic of Korea
- Singapore
- Spain
- Switzerland
- Taiwan
- USA
- United Kingdom

If you hold a passport from Thailand or Brunei, you will only be given a 15-day visa when you arrive.

If your country is not on the list, it's always a good idea to check with your local embassy website to find out more. If any case, always check online for up to date information, as visa information and requirements can and do change quite regularly.

In addition to the temporary visa you will be given at the airport, there might be a few other requirements that you should ring with you. Remember, immigration staff can ask you questions about your intentions in Japan if they see fit, and in that case, simply be honest and explain that you're visiting for a vacation and for sightseeing. You may be asked for evidence of a return flight ticket, e.g. the day you're going to leave Japan. Some officers ask for this, other's don't; it's really a case of 'what happens on the day'.

There is also a chance wherein you will be asked to show proof that you can afford to fund your visit. When asked for this, a credit card, money, or a bank statement would be enough. It's rare to be asked for this, but it's simply a case of being prepared.

We would also like point out that everyone who enters Japan should have their photograph taken and as well as their fingerprints. This will be done when you arrive at the airport. Your visa will be scanned and stamped with your visitors' visa. This is the standard practice in Japan and there is nothing to worry about.

Chapter 4:
JAPAN TOURIST SPOTS – TOWNS AND CITIES NOT TO MISS!

Japan is far larger than you might think, and there are so many things to see and do in those four islands! It's very unlikely that you will get to see everything during your time there unless you're planning on using up your full 90-day tourist visa to get around Japan on your own steam!

The first place that most people think of when they hear the word 'Japan' is without a doubt Tokyo. This is a huge and bustling city, one which will leave you awestruck, but you should explore the other cities too. In this chapter, we are going to talk about the famous spots in Japan that you need to add on your must-visit list.

First, we have to talk about the neon lights of Tokyo.

Let's Talk Tokyo

Many people arrive in Japan through one of Tokyo's famous airports which is located in the main island of Honshu.

Most people consider Tokyo to be huge, far too congested, and a total head spin. In some ways they are correct, but if you look a little further beyond the hustle and bustle, you'll actually see a lot of history and culture too. This is a city which has a wonderful blend of the past and the modern day.

Of course, there are lots of skyscrapers and high-tech spots, and that is actually what Tokyo is known for all over the world. But, you'll also find places like the Meiji Shinto Shrine and huge woods, and the opulent Imperial Palace and large gardens. For a chill-out or a break from the craziness of the city center, these gardens are really a refreshing sight to see.

We know that Tokyo is the capital city and that means that you'll find all the modern-day amenities there, as well as shopping stores. But know that, when you splurge, you are likely to max out on your credit card limit, especially if you head to Roppongi Hills which is a huge entertainment and shopping complex.

Most people who arrive in Tokyo immediately panic about how they're going to get around, but it is surprisingly easy. The subway is very easy to use, and you can purchase a pre-paid travel card at any station. During rush hour, however, the Subway can be EXTREMELY busy. So, if you want convenience, then you can take a taxi to bring you to places. But, this mode of transportation can get very expensive, so you'd better try to avoid it.

Tokyo is also the world's most populous city, so you can expect a lot of people walking with you when going down the street. There are several districts within the city that you can check out. If you're into history and want to get away from the busy city life for like an hour or so, you can visit Asakusa. It is a place where you can wander around air-conditioned museums and visit many temples, such as the Sensoji Temple. In the Northern Tokyo area, you should also head to Rikugien, which is a traditional Japanese garden full of shaded areas.

Put simply, if you visit Japan and don't spend a few days at the very least in Tokyo, you will miss a lot. Go to the top of the Tokyo Skytree, at 634 meters tall, and enjoy the panoramic view of one of the busiest cities in the world. There is also an aquarium at the bottom of the tower too. Of course, there is Tokyo Disneyland which is a short distance from the city.

There is by far too much to see and do in Tokyo. So, if you're visiting Japan, Tokyo should be on your priority list and spend a few days at the very least. This is considered as one of the world's most famous cities, so better not miss it.

It's Not All About the Capital

Aside from the city capital, Japan has many other small towns and cities that are also worth visiting. To give you an idea on where they are located, check out this quick guide below.

- **Hokkaido Island.** This is the northern island, which is literally opposite the coast of Russia! As a result, you can expect freezing cold winters and snowy scenes, but this is also where you'll find Japan's premier ski resorts, such as Furano Ski Resort, Rusutsu Resort, and Sapporo Teine.
- **Honshu Island, Tohoku.** This is the northeast part of the main Honshu Island and is a great spot to know more about the traditional way of life in more rural settings. If you love seafood, this is a great spot to go to, but in the winter you can also ski here, thanks to its northern location. Hot springs are plentiful around here too but remember if you have tattoos, you're might

struggle to get in! In this region, you will find Yamagata, Fukushima, Miyagi, and Akita.

- **Honshu Island, Kanto.** This is the part of the main island where Tokyo is located, as well as Yokohama, which is another top spot to visit. Kanto runs along the coast, so during the summer months, you'll find beaches quite busy, as locals head there on weekends. Around 100km away from Tokyo, you will also find the iconic Mount Fuji, an active volcano which is popular for hiking.
- **Honshu Island, Chibu.** This area is home to the city of Nagoya, but also encompasses Nagano, Shizuoka, and Ishikawa too. The Japan Alps are found here, so you can certainly expect dramatic landscapes and photo opportunities! This is an inland area, located in the center of the main Honshu Island.
- **Honshu Island, Kansai.** This part of Honshu is home to Osaka, another huge city and place to visit if you want to explore more. Kyoto and Nara are also here, as well as Kobe. This region is located in the west of Honshu and has plenty of cultural hotspots to check out.
- **Honshu Island, Chugoku.** Historians would want to head to the Chugoku area, as it is where you will find Okayama and Hiroshima. Here you see find the Hiroshima Peace Memorial Park, which commemorates the victims of the atomic bomb in 1945. This is an area of countryside, but there are many beautiful spots to head to, including Mount Wisen and Itsukushima, a coastal region with laidback beaches.
- **Shikoku Island.** This is the smallest of the islands and it is mostly where you will see people heading for either white water rafting (fantastic conditions), to visit Takamatsu and Matsuyama (two big cities), or when visiting as part of a Buddhist pilgrimage. Due to the natural setting, you can expect some amazing views here.
- **Kyushu Island.** This island is where most people deem Japanese civilization to have been born, and here you will find Fukuoka and Kitakyushu, as the two largest cities in the region. Kyushu

is located in the most southern part of the main Japanese islands, and one of the must-visits is Beppu, which has a cable car going up to Mt. Tsurumi where you will see amazing views.

- **Okinawa.** This is a chain of islands that covers south of Japan and towards Taiwan. These islands are semitropical and as a result have much warmer weather, which can become very humid during the summer months. There are 49 islands which are inhabited, with regular domestic flights from the mainland, and 111 which are uninhabited. Most people head to Okinawa for its amazing beaches that are great for snorkeling.

How to Travel Around Japan

The fact that Japan is a chain of islands means that if you want to venture from one island to another, you are obviously going to need to fly or take the ferry. Thankfully, island hopping in Japan is a very easy and a fun thing to do!

Japan has a state-of-the-art train system, but buses are your best bet if you want to get around Hokkaido's national parks and the smaller islands. Buses are also a lot cheaper than trains, so this is an excellent option if you are traveling on a tight budget.

Traveling by Air

Japan is a big country. So, if you have limited time, then flying is the best way to get around and see more. You can book for domestic flight tickets and grab the lowest fares. Haneda Airport in Tokyo serves both international and domestic flights. The two main Japanese airlines that cover domestic flights are Japan Airlines and All Nippon Airways. You can also find cheaper rates with airlines like Skymark and Jetstar Japan.

To give you an idea about distance and traveling time, a domestic flight from Tokyo to the beaches in Okinawa – it will take an average of 2 hours and 15 minutes.

Traveling by Train

The train is a quick way to travel around Japan and covers all the main islands. The bullet train, hits a speed of up to 200 miles an hour, so you will be in your destination sooner than you thought! Meals are also being served when you're traveling by train, most of the time you will get something called 'ekiben'; this is a food box that contains food that is popular in the region that you are going to visit.

Trains in Japan are rarely late. In fact, they're amongst the most punctual in the world. They're also very clean, and you can shop around to find the best deals quite easily. Foreign visitors can also look into train passes dedicated to tourists, with the Japan Rail Pass a good idea. If you're considering traveling around Japan in this way, a rail pass will keep Yen in your pocket.

There are also some train trips which you can take to show you the best sceneries that Japan has to offer, such as between Akita and Aomori. It will take you through the stunning Shirakami Range.

Traveling by Bus

Long-distance coaches cover most of Japan and are a comfortable and cheap way to get around. Some overnight buses have seats which recline so you can get a good night's sleep, and this is a good option if trains aren't available where you are going (e.g. more rural areas), or if you're looking to save cash.

Do bear in mind that if you have a large amount of luggage, the coach may refuse to carry it, if they don't have space.

Traveling by Ferry

We've talked about how to get to Japan by ferry from neighboring countries, but the ferry is also a very easy and useful way to get around the country's main islands if you want to do the more laidback route. Do bear in mind that traveling by ferry could eat a lot of time, like the Kagoshima to Naha ferry which can take up to 25 hours! If you're not pressed on time and you want to see the coastal areas, then taking the ferry is a good option.

You will be able to find up to date information on travel time, routes, and fares online, as these may change on a regular basis. Also bear in mind that during bad weather, ferries are usually the first mode of transportation that closes temporarily, it will resume operation once the weather is clear.

Traveling by Car

If you want to hire a car, you can. But, you may have a hard time because most of the road signs are in Japanese. Otherwise, you will need an English GPS to help you get from point A to point B. You must also provide an International Driver's License, and you will be asked to show both the paper and card.

You can hire a car in any major city, through companies like Nippon Rent a Car, Avis, and Toyota Rent a Car.

Now, you know how to get from point A to B, let's move to the fun stuff, the things that you should see and do!

Chapter 4:
THINGS TO SEE AND DO

We have talked about all the traveling details when in Japan and you should be feeling pretty excited and prepared now that we've got this far. So, let's make it even more exciting by talking about the amazing things that you can see and do in this amazing country.

Some of the main activities that you should not miss out on during your stay are the following:

Climb Mount Fuji – Yes, you read that right! Mount Fuji is one of the most iconic sights in all of Japan, and it's entirely possible to climb it and have one of the most emotional moments of your life. The sights before you will blow your mind. The best times to climb are between July until mid-September and be prepared with all supplies, comfortable clothing and supportive footwear. Before you panic, this isn't actually a very difficult climb, but there are a few areas which are quite steep. The biggest problems are the crowds! The sunrise is truly amazing too.

Visit Arashiyama Monkey Park in Iwatayama – Kyoto is home to the cheekiest monkeys around, and here you play with them and interact safely. This is a great spot for flies and those who simply love animals too.

Check Out The Cherry Blossom – Visit between March to April and you will see the beautiful cherry blossom in full bloom! This is known as 'hanami,' roughly translated as 'flower viewing' and you sit under the trees and look up. It's a peaceful and beautiful way to spend an afternoon in peace and quiet.

Head to a Sumo Wrestling Match – Of course, this is the national sport and whilst you might find watching a grown man in a makeshift diaper fight with another man rather odd, it's something you should experience! Tokyo is the place to see this, but you can also watch similar shows in other main towns and cities.

Visit the Hiroshima Peace Memorial Museum – Located inside a national park, you will find a museum that is dedicated to all the victims of the devastating atomic bomb which fell in this very spot. You will find this to be a very busy spot, as people head here to pray and wish for peace worldwide.

Learn at the National Museum of Emerging Science and Innovation – Located in central part of Tokyo, this museum might not be something you would want to put on your list immediately, but give it a chance, because it's one of the most visited attractions and for a very good reason! You'll learn more about science and technology here such as robots and outer space. It is also a great place to take the kids.

Enjoy Peace and Quiet at Kenrokuen – Located in Ishikawa, Kendrokuen is a stunning spot, full of lakes, trees, small bridges, fountains, and old buildings. It's a spot where you won't be able to feel any type of stress or worry at all! The leaves change color according to the season, and autumn is a very colorful time to visit, with bright orange everywhere you look.

Head to The Top of the Skytree – We've already mentioned that Tokyo's premier viewing spot is at the top of the Skytree and this is certainly a must do you need on your list. You can easily view the entirety of this huge city from the viewing area. Possibly not one for those with a fear of heights, however!

Visit Kawachi Fuji Gardens – Head to Fukuoka if you love lavenders and purples, as this garden will blow your mind. You can even walk through a dome of flowers which leaves you emerged in nature. Head there at the end of April, into the second week of May for the brightest colors.

Check Out the Penguins at Hokkaido Zoo – We've already mentioned that Hokkaido is a cold place, but that is the ideal spot for checking out the entertaining penguins and seals at Asahiyama Zoo!

Sing Karaoke – This is something you should try! You'll find countless Karaoke bars all over the main cities, but the biggest ones are obviously in Tokyo. Go ahead, grab that mic and sing!

Head to Shibuya and Check Out the 'Scramble Intersection' – You probably saw a blurred picture of what seems like thousands of people crossing the road with the neon-lit Tokyo buildings in front. This is the 'scramble interaction' and it is located in Shibuya. Head to the top floor of Starbucks and gaze through the window for the best view of this chaotic road crossing!

Visit an Animal Cafe – Tokyo, in particular, has many animal cafes, and these are literally what they sound like; a cafe where you enjoy a drink and pet animals! There is an owl cafe, a hedgehog cafe, and the list goes on.

Explore Sensoji Temple – Located in the Asakusa region of Tokyo, this is one of the most famous temples in Japan and a very popular place to visit.

Remember to always adhere to temple etiquette, as this is a sacred spot especially to the locals. As you walk up to the entrance of the temple, you will find many vendors selling street foods, so be sure to give those a try too!

Check Out Tsukiji Fish Market – Another Tokyo attraction is the huge Tsukiji Fish Market, where you'll find all manner of seafood to try, kitchen gadgets and the famous Tuna Auction. Of course, you should definitely try some sushi here, especially if it's your first time!

Visit Arashiyama Bamboo Forest – Arashiyama is a large city, but as you venture towards it, either by road or by train, you'll go through the towering stalks bamboo which makes up the famous bamboo forest. It's a definite must see and really quite wonderful.

Experience Fushimi Inari – Kyoto is home to the serene and wonderful Fushimi Inari shrine, which has gates in bright colors and corridors to wander through. Remember to adhere to shrine etiquette, as we spoke about earlier, but this is certainly one of the most popular shrines in all of Japan.

Ski in Hokkaido – Between November and February you can ski to your heart's content at several resorts on Hokkaido. Ideal for beginners, intermediates, and advanced abilities, there are also children's schools here for the little ones if you are bringing a kid with you.

Visit Jigokudani National Park and Say Hello to The Macaque Snow Monkeys – These are downright beautiful little animals, but they're hardy, as they can live in minus 15 degrees± This park is where you will get to see them, during the winter months.

Tokyo's Imperial Palace – The Imperial family still live here, and this is a true sign of Tokyo's history and culture. You can wander around the grounds and the beautifully kept gardens, and during the Emperor's Birthday celebrations and New Year, you can even go inside the palace.

Buy some Tech in Akihabara - If you're after the latest technological gadget, or you're a fan of anime, then you have to go to Akihabara, a part of Tokyo. This is a hugely busy, bustling, and neon-lit spot, packed with more stores than you can possibly visit during even a week!

Experience Manga at a Manga Kissa (cafe) - Here you can read and experience the art of manga and anime in full force. It's all going to be in Japanese, which is something you should be aware of, but the experience is pretty cool!

The Robot Restaurant Dining Experience - In terms of experience, this is one you must have, but you might not understand! Hugely popular, you will certainly need to book your tickets beforehand, but this is basically a dinner show in Tokyo, which talks about robots, science fiction, and all other weirdness. Strange, but quite compelling!

Go to a Kabuki Show - This is a cultural experience you need to have and it is a traditional type of art which has roots as far back as Edo times. This is a show which is done by men and is a theatrical performance with costumes and a window to the old type of Japan you might not be aware still exists.

Gaze in Awe at Himeji Castle - This is one of the country's 12 castles which is still standing and hasn't been damaged or fallen due to an earthquake or another issue. You'll sometimes hear this called the White Heron Castle and it is stunning. Dating back to the 1400s, the castle was a fortress to guard Kyoto, but nowadays it's simply a sign of architecture and wonder.

Experience a Buddhist Retreat - There are many temples which offer Buddhists retreats, but Mount Koya has one of the most popular and serene. You can learn about Buddhist monks, and this type of retreat will give you more access to the temple, as you will be able to walk around the grounds freely.

Okinawa's Scuba Diving Opportunities - As the most southern point of Japan, this is a truly beautiful spot for beach time, but also for checking out the marine life of the area too. The water is impossibly blue here, and you'll find many different diving spots, such as diving from the shore, reefs in shallow water, to deeper drop-offs. If you're an experienced diver, you certainly won't be disappointed here either.

Visit Kinkaku-Ji Temple - If you want one of the most jaw-dropping sceneries for your picture taking, this is the one you're looking for! Surrounded by hills, greenery, and reflected perfectly in the water, this temple is located in Kyoto and is designed in gold left. Whilst Japan has many temples, this is certainly one of the most Instagrammable!

Let Your Hair Down on The Golden Gai - Tokyo's oldest and most famous bar crawl is called the Golden Gai, and here you will be able to drink yourself into what can only be described as an alcoholic stupor. The Golden Gai consists of six alleyways which contain chilled out bars which have an old-world feel to them.

Love Cats? Go to Cat Island - If you're a cat lover, it has to be Tashirojima for you! This is an island where there are more cats than people, by about 6 to 1! This used to be a small fishing island, but nowadays cat lovers flock in their droves. Despite that, it is a little off the beaten track and doesn't have a huge amount of facilities, so be prepared when going there.

Go Hiking in The Northern Alps - If total natural emersion is your thing, the Northern Alps are for you. These begin at Kamikochi Resort in Chubu Sangak National Park and within the area, you can hike either on beginner's trails, or head to some more challenging treks, which take several days to complete. There are camping sites around here too and you'll certainly get plenty of fresh mountain air!

We could keep going, but we'd still be talking by the time you're thinking of heading off to the airport! These are just some of the things that you should not miss and the more obscure and off the beaten track activities to enjoy while you are in Japan.

Why You Have to Try Japanese Food?

There is one thing we haven't talked about yet, and it is a huge and integral part of any visit to Japan – the FOOD!

Yes, Japanese cuisine is definitely a must-try. If you haven't tried sushi before or didn't like it the first time you tried, then this is the best place to give it another shot because by far it is a lot better in Japan!

Of course, there are western-style restaurants in the big cities, with Tokyo certainly having the major fast food chains. But, why not let your taste buds have an adventure of its own? You can have a McDonalds at any time, but can you try authentic Japanese food at any time? Of course not!

In general, Japanese cuisine is based on the ingredients that are in season. This way, they get to serve fresh and delicious food which is mostly made up of rice, noodles, meat, and vegetables. Seafood is also a big thing in Japan, and various dishes use seafood as a main ingredient like Tempura, Sushi, Sashimi, and a lot more.

If you don't know where to start or what food to try, here are some of the must-try dishes that you shouldn't miss.

- **Sushi and Sashimi** – We will link these two together because they are very similar. Sushi is obviously rice and vegetables, with fish and wrapped in nori. There are countless types of sushi, and in every single town or city, you'll find countless of sushi bars so better check them out. On the other hand, sashimi is a slice of raw fish which is served with soy sauce and wasabi; beware of wasabi - it's spicy!
- **Ramen** - Certainly one of the most iconic dishes in Japan, you'll hear people slurping their ramen noodles noisily, and it's something you should join in! These noodles are wheat noodles, and they have miso

soup with them or soy sauce. You'll also find other types of ingredients, sometimes shrimp, onions, egg, or seaweed. Truly delicious and very filling.

- **Tempura** – There is no doubt that you have tried this before or at least heard of it, but tempura is a type of street food that can be served in many ways. The food is deep-fried and it can be made of anything, from vegetables to different types of seafood. Whilst tempura is fried, it feels dry, so it's not greasy, and is quite light. You can also choose from a wide variety of dips.

- **Kare-Raisu** - Warm and filling, this is basically Japanese curry with rice, but it's not the type of curry you'll have had in India or in China. You'll find carrots, peas, mushrooms and all other types of vegetables within the curry, and different meats, including duck and beef, pork, or chicken. You can go for the hottest or you can go mild, the choice is yours!

- **Miso Soup** - Never tried miso soup? Now is the time to try it! This is usually served as a side dish, but you can go for it as a snack too. Miso is made of fermented soybeans, so they're very good for you, and you'll often find tofu, onion, seaweed, vegetables and other ingredients inside. You'll be served a side of rice with it, but you'll never be given miso as your main meal.

- **Yakitori** - Probably one of the easiest among the Japanese foods for first-time visitors, yakitori is a skewer of meat, usually beef or fish. These are brushed with sticky teriyaki sauce. Yakitori is usually eaten as a fast food option, it is like eating a kebab after a night out!

- **Onigiri** - This is a very popular snack dish and you'll find it anywhere. Onigiri is basically a ball of seasoned rice. But, some have meat inside or vegetables. A quick grab and go food for people in a hurry.

Chapter 5:
BUDGET TIPS - SAVE CASH
AND SEE MORE

As you can see, Japan has a lot to offer, no matter where you choose to stay, which also means you need enough money to be able to see the best of it.

Visiting Japan can certainly be expensive if you choose to go to all the major tourist destinations and travel around constantly. Tokyo alone can be super expensive if you decide to shop 'til you drop and stay in expensive hotels or eat in restaurants most of the time. Just like in any country, you can make your travel to Japan expensive or low-cost as possible.

In this chapter, we will give you a few final tips on how to save cash while seeing more.

- **Make use of rail passes**. Yes, the bullet trains are a tourist attraction themselves, but they're not the cheapest way to get around. You can purchase a rail pass and use the regular trains, or you can go by bus and save cash that way too.
- **Travel indirect**. Before you even get to Japan, think about flying indirect to save cash on your airfare. This is probably going to be the most expensive part of your break, so any cash saved here can be put to good use elsewhere.
- **Buy a Metro pass in Tokyo**. Another transport money saver is to buy a day-long Metro pass (subway) in Tokyo and use it for the entire day without having to pay every time.
- **Avoid the tourist restaurants**. You will find many restaurants that target tourists, and you will know this because the prices are extremely higher! If you love sushi, you can expect to pay a fair amount of cash. However, you can also eat in traditional restaurants that also serve great food at reasonable prices. Simply ask a hotel member or staff where they eat, or wander around yourself and see where most of the locals eat. As a side point, if you do love sushi and you want to save cash, sushi trains are where it's at!
- **Stay in hostels**. Most hostels are inexpensive in Japan and will save you a lot compared to hotels. Some even allow you to stay for free if you do a spot of cleaning!
- **Purchase Kyoto's temple pass**. If you want to explore several temples in the Kyoto area, you can buy the temple pass which will save you plentiful cash throughout your stay, and it also includes transport to the temples themselves.
- **Check out the free attractions**. Most gardens and temples offer free entrance. Look for more of this and mix them with the paid for attractions.

- **Give yourself a budget.** It can be very easy to overspend in Japan and there's no denying that it can really be expensive if you will splurge. Set yourself a budget and better stick with it!

These are just some of the best ways to save cash whilst visiting Japan. Of course, Japan isn't the cheapest country in the world, but it's certainly not the most expensive either. Your biggest expenses will be for traveling and food, but there are many others as well, as we have outlined in this section, and throughout the book.

Avoid spending too much on novelty items, because that is where many people lose their Yen! Tokyo, in particular, is packed with small stores where many visitors buy these souvenirs because they're different and make great gifts for people back home. Better watch out. Otherwise, you'll lose a lot of cash by doing this!

It's also a good idea to simply take as many photos as you can and use these as your personal souvenir. You don't need to buy expensive stuff, memories are far more important, especially in a place like this.

Conclusion

And there we have it, everything you need to know to start planning your trip to Japan.

By this point, you should be full of excitement to go to Japan because you are now armed with all the information you need to have a memorable time. Moreover, you already know how to save money to make the most out of your travel in the Land of the Rising Sun.

Remember to check first the visa requirements before you go. This book provided you the most up to date information, but this can be updated on a regular basis. You should also check the ferry rates and their operation hours if you're planning on traveling around the country by sea.

It is now easier to visit Japan than it has ever been before, and the good thing is that despite an increased number of visitors, the country remains peace and order. You can easily see the western influence in terms of fast food joints, but the culture of Japan is still vibrant and unique.

Remember that Japan is extremely different to anywhere else which you might have visited in the past. Explore and enjoy every minute of it. Take as many photographs as you can to capture all those precious moments, because this is going to be a one vacation that you will never forget!